BOSH BLOBBER BOSH

Runcible Poems for Edward Lear by J. P

BOSH BLOI

Creative Editions,

atrick Lewis · Illustrations by Gary Kelley

BBER BOSH

Mankato, Minnesota

For Edward Lear
il miglior fabbro

J. P. L.

•

For My Uncle Eugene
who handed me my first pencil

G. R. K.

List of Poems

Born in a Crowd

The Creatures Wearing Clothes

The Queen Takes Drawing Lessons

Letter by Numbers to His Friend, Chichester Fortescue

A Day in the Life . . .

. . . A Night in the Life

Aboard the SS Coffee-Cup

In the Middle of Your Face

"There once was a man who could cook"

"There was an Old Man of Dundee"

"That man with the battering ram'll"

"There once was a man who loved vowels"

Finding Paradise (and Losing It)

The Earl of Derby and The Book of Nonsense

Old Foss (the Cat) Recalls His Life with Mr. Lear

In the Kingdom of Lear

Introduction

THERE ONCE was an Englishman by the name of Edward Lear who claimed he was "perfectly spherical" and who wore "a runcible hat." He had a big nose, a bald head, a bushy beard, and twenty brothers and sisters. He never married, though he was very much in love with a Jumbly girl and a Lady Jingly, neither of whom existed. Friends? Oh, he had many friends, but Mr. Lear spent most of his life alone with Giorgio, his servant, and Foss, his ever-faithful cat.

Together they sailed away to real worlds like Italy and Egypt, Greece and Corsica. But what he loved most of all was to roam the world of make-believe he himself created. Places like Lake Pipple-Popple, the Torrible Zone, the Chankly Bore, and the Great Gromboolian Plain.

Except for dogs (which he hated) and camels (which hated him), Mr. Lear loved animals. You may remember him as the inventor of "The Owl and the Pussy-Cat," "The Courtship of the Yonghy-Bonghy-Bò," "The Jumblies," and many other nonsense poems, songs, and limericks. But he also invented Oblong Oysters, the Biscuit Buffalo, the Quangle Wangle, and many. . .

Quangle Wangle? Lake Pipple-Popple? If you had heard this story a century ago (when it actually happened), you might have said, "Oh, bosh!"

Exactly. Bosh is nonsense. And Edward Lear is one of the greatest Bosh inventors of all time.

What is so amazing about him is that he filled the lives of others with laughter, even though his own life was marked by illness and unhappiness. He suffered from asthma, rheumatism, and from the age of seven until his death at seventy-five in 1888, epilepsy—the "Terrible Demon" he called it.

"It is a blessing," he said, "that I have not gone utterly to the bad mad sad."

Still in his twenties, Mr. Lear became one of England's best-known painters of birds—colorful and detailed "pigchers" of exotic cockatoos, parrots, and macaws. But whether to forget his loneliness or to find adventure, he left England and took up the life of a wanderer, painting nature in strange and faraway lands. At fifty-nine, he moved to San Remo, Italy, where he lived the last seventeen years of his life, still traveling as often as his failing health would allow.

Now Victorian England, which had been Mr. Lear's home, could be stuffy and starched and all too serious. So he invented his own world of Bosh, complete with chocolate shrimps and lovely monkeys with lollipop paws. Gosky patties and calico pies. Bong trees and runcible spoons. Whenever he was at a loss for words, he simply made up new ones. "Spongetaneous" and "splitmecrackle" words that can enchant children (and adults) as much today as they did a hundred years ago.

There is no map of Mr. Lear's world; none is needed. Travel past Dingle Bank, over the Tiniskoop Hills, down through the Valley of Verrikwier to the Syllabub Sea—or go in precisely the opposite direction—and you'll come to a magical place of cockeyed words and laughter: the land of high Bosh.

Boshblobberbosh is not really a life story—there are several excellent biographies already available. This book of poems is a way of tipping a runcible hat and swashbuckling a grateful bow to the memory of a poet in return for the many pleasures he has given readers the world over. Some of the poems are based on actual events; some cross over the line into Bosh territory. But all of the poems are meant to honor one of the world's great word-wizards and nonsense poets, "that crazy old Englishman, oh!"—Edward Lear.

J. P. L.

Now I was my mother's twentieth child

(Another one came after me!).

Some of my sisters were mannered and mild,

Some of my brothers were wicked and wild.

But I was my mother's twentieth child—

She couldn't look after me.

Well, I was my father's fourth or fifth boy.

He wanted so much to be rich,

And once he bought me a marvelous toy

That only time and neglect would destroy.

For I was my father's fourth or fifth boy—

He couldn't remember which.

I was just like a son to my sister Ann

(Which made her a mother to me).

Often we romped in the meadows and ran

To the green leaf trees where a world began.

I was just like a son to my sister Ann,

Who always looked after me.

She always looked after me.

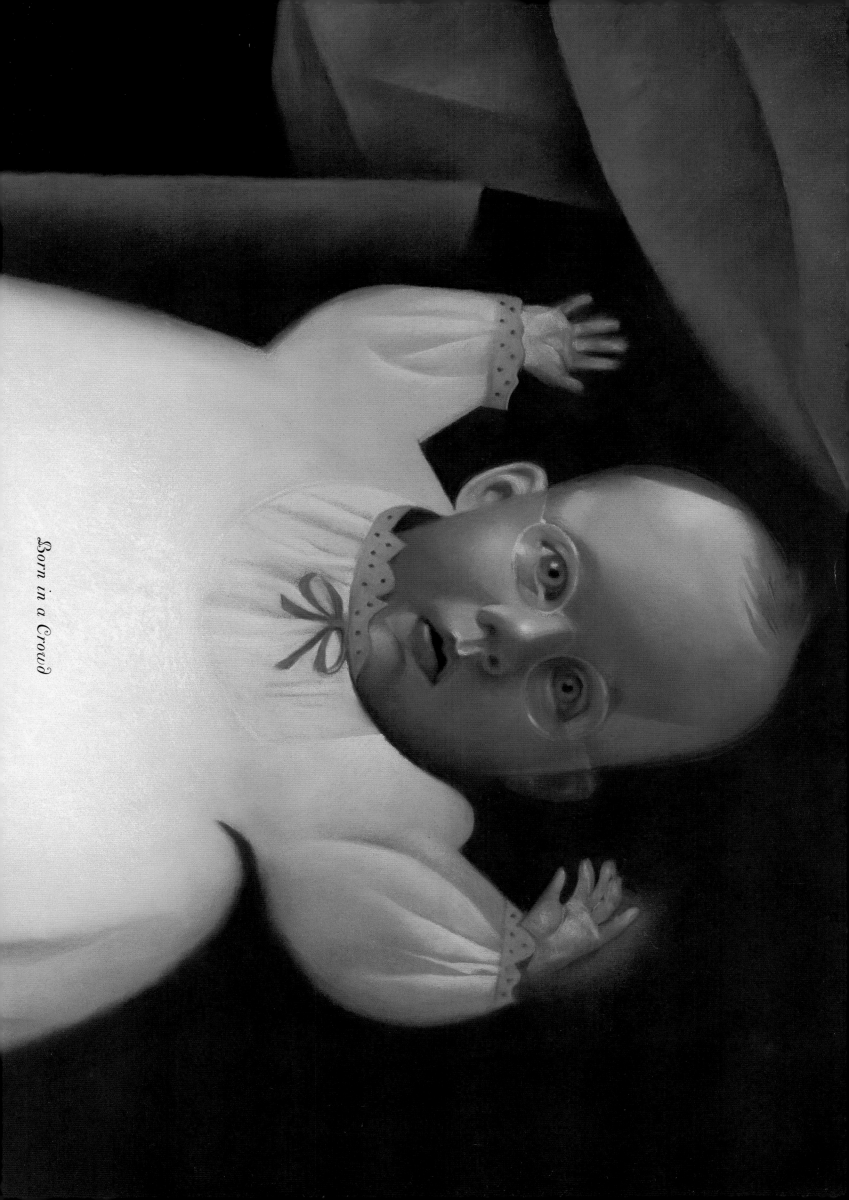

Born in a Crowd

The Creatures Wearing Clothes

The Zoo at Regent's Park
On Sunday afternoons
Resembles Noah's Ark.
Large Families of Baboons,
Giraffes, and Crocodiles
Line up in perfect rows
To smile toothy smiles
At creatures wearing clothes.

And in the House of Birds
The Parrots also pose,
But what excites the herds
(Of creatures wearing clothes)
Is perched upon a limb—
A Parrot-painting lad!
And while they gawk at him,
He doodles on a pad.

Some holler toward the tree,
"Poor boy, he's flipped his lid!"
While others jump to see
The doodle that he did
Of feather, beak, and claw.
But just before he goes,
He settles back to draw
A creature wearing clothes!

The Queen Takes Drawing Lessons

At Buckingham Palace in royal red
    The Queen of England drew
A picture of herself, and said,
    "Now tell me, tell me true!"
Her Lords began to weep because
Each knew exactly *what* it was
    But none of them knew *who*!

The first one cried, "Beef Stroganoff!"
    The second said, "Hyena!"
The third exclaimed, "It's slightly off—
    The Coast of Argentina!"
The more they wept, the more they guessed—
    "Potatoes in their skin?"
"A Tuning Fork!" "A Buzzard's Nest!"
    "The Duke of Wellington?"

"You nincompoops!" the royal jaw
    Shot back, and cracked the chandelier.
"I'll have you know I learned to draw
    From Master Mr. Lear.
Go fetch the famous lad for me!"
Her Lords looked up. "Your Majesty,
    He's standing in the rear."

As Lear approached the Head of State,
    He saw that quirk of art
And thought of . . . Beef upon a Plate?!
    It nearly broke his heart.
But all he said was "Ah, my Queen?"
    And fell into her lap
As large and lean as the Argentine.
    She smiled. "You clevah chap!"

EDWARD LEAR

2345 PIPPLE-POPPLE LANE
CHANKLY BORE, ENGLAND

Letter by Numbers to His Friend,
Chichester Fortescue

My Dear 4Oscue:

I'm off 2 seek my 4chun with the sunrise—
They say the weather's gr8 in Timbuk2.
I hope 2 paint 16y-weeny butterflies
And catch a cagey cocka2 4 you.

Though overw8, I long 4 the sensation
Of flying like we of1O flew last year.
But cocka2s size up the situation—
1 1ders how 2 nab this souvenir.
If 5 dumb luck, you'll see me at the station
With bird in hand.

Yours Ever,
Edward Lear

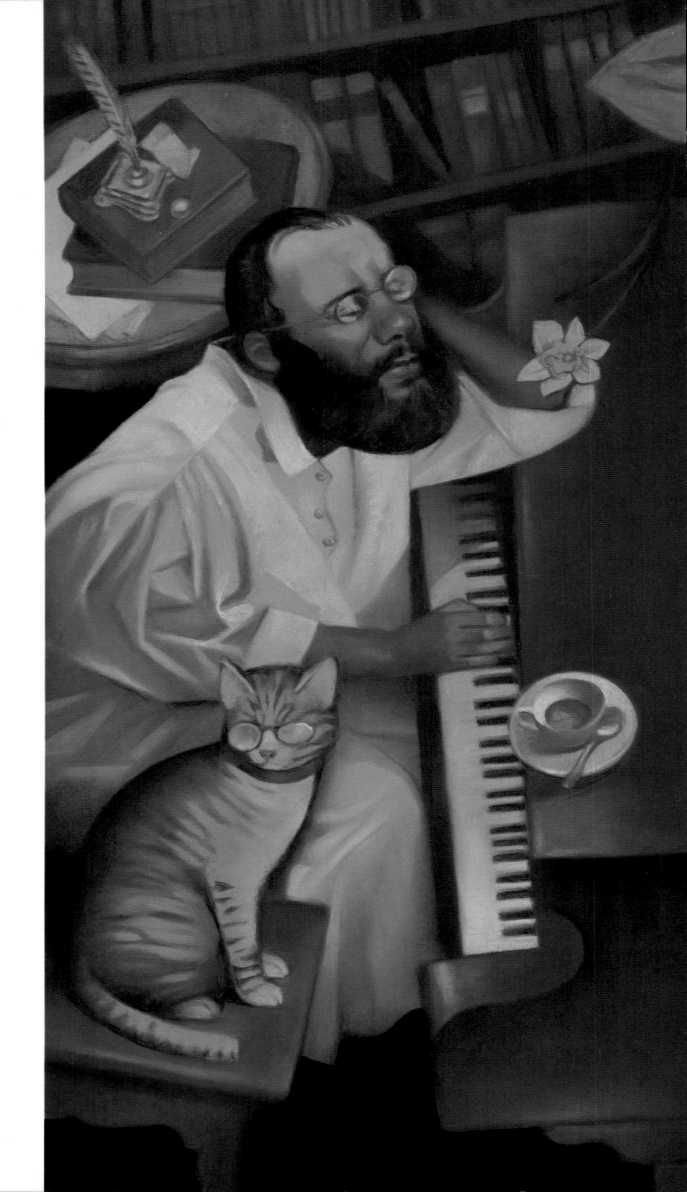

A Day in the Life . . .

Mr. Lear
Wakes at ten
Walks six miles
Paints a glen
Points his cat
Home again

Picks an olive
Plucks a flower
Takes a bath
By thundershower
Hears the cuckoo
Cluck the hour

So at four
Sips his tea
Takes a nap
Later he
Tickles high
Society

Pats his bed
Snuggles in
Opens mail
With a grin
Reads a book
By Tennyson

Lays it down
Wonders long
Understands
What is wrong
Hums a little
Silly song

Hums a little
Silly song
Hums a little
Silly . . .

. . . A Night in the Life

. . . the silly song
That he hears
Dims the dark
Demon fears
Through this night
Of Mr. Lear's

Down the wind
Wizards coast
On floating rugs
Of buttered toast
To the white
Night-gowned host

Take the painter
By the hand
Sail away
To Popple Land
Dancing to
A Rubber Band

Suddenly
A daffodil
Hops along
His windowsill
To a snappy
Tune until

Lady Jingly
Dressed in blue
Throws a kiss
Maybe two
Mr. Bosh
One's for you

Comes the dawn
Tilly-loo
Lady Jingly
Where are you?

Aboard the SS _Coffee-Cup_

"Must we splish and splash about?"
    Said the Salmon to the Trout,
"Why, we're causing such commotion
    That it's steaming up the ocean!"

Said the kindly Trout, "Examine
    That horizon, Mr. Salmon,
And you'll see what's steaming up—
    It's the SS _Coffee-Cup!_"

Then they leaped through choppy seas
    Crying out, "Come join us, please!"
Lear could read a fish's lips
    And he loved those deep-sea dips,

But he said, "I've got the chills
    For I've lost my swimming pills!"
So the fish, a moment later,
    Somersaulted up the freighter.

"Meet my Cat, Old Foss, who serves
    The most naughtical hors d'oeuvres."
Said the host, "Oh, won't you stay?"
    Said the Salmon, "Not today!"

"Th-Th-Thank you," said the Trout,
"But C-Cats can do without
    Our delicious company!"
    And the fish flipped back to sea.

As they tumbled topsy-turvy,
    Mr. Salmon said, "How nervy . . .
Just imagine . . . Have you _ever!?_"
    Mr. Trout said, "No, I _never!_"

And across the ocean deep
    (Mr. Lear began to weep,
    Mr. Foss began to cry),
    Came the echo of a sigh:

    "G-G-Good b-b-b-bye!"

In the Middle

Do you often take for granted
Something that is squarely planted
Sometimes straight but mostly slanted
In the middle of your face?

Think how often you'd surprise
Neighbors with your flat disguise
If nothing separates your eyes
In the middle of your face.

of Your Face

It's impossible to speak

(Or dance alone, yes, cheek-to-cheek)

If there is nothing left to tweak

In the middle of your face

So be grateful for your nose

Because it's just where it's supposed

To be for taking all those blows

In the middle of your face

*T*HERE ONCE was a man
who could cook

But he ate everything in the book

From the rack of lamb

To the hock of ham

And it gave him a spherical look.

When the Jumblies arrived at the door,

He invited them in but he swore,

"A party this big

Will require a Pig,

And I fear it would be such a Bore!"

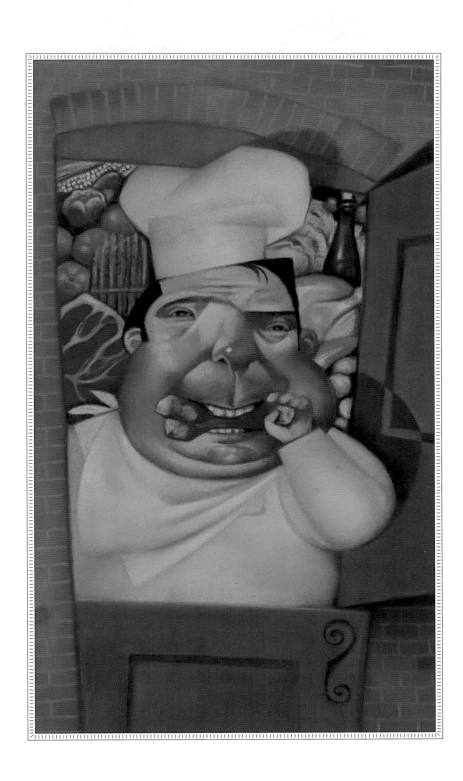

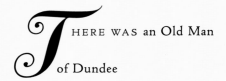

*T*HERE WAS an Old Man
of Dundee

Who threw Cranberry Tarts in the sea;

The Fizzgiggious Fish

Thought the dish was delish,

Though they much preferred

crumpets and tea.

And that Man of Dundee, on a whim,

Dove in for an afternoon swim

With the Mackerel crowd

Who kept crying out loud,

For the Fish are just wild about him.

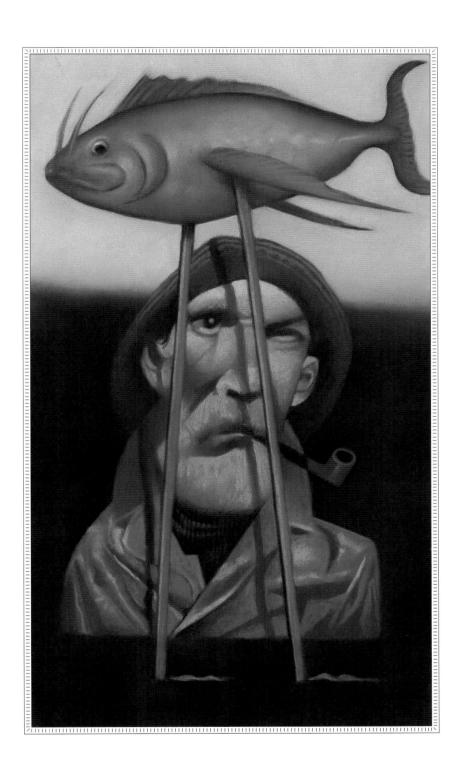

*T*HAT MAN with the

battering ram'll

Try to flatten the hump on his camel;

For he says, "It's a crime

When a painter must climb

Up the peak of a pokey old mammal!"

*T*HERE ONCE was a man
who loved vowels

So much that he hooted to owls.

When they cried, "Ooo-ooo-ooh!"

He cried, "Ooo-ooh! to you,

You half-moony meloobious fowls!"

Finding Paradise
(and Losing It)

Mr. Lear had widely traveled
But the roads he took were graveled
    And his pheet were getting sore.
So he thought it wise to settle
Where a Pobble wouldn't pedal—
Where the Jumblies like to meddle—
    In the Hills of Chankly Bore.

Then the phriendly Rural Raven
Phlew him to a happy haven
    On the phar Italian shore.
To the coast he made a beeline
With his phat and phavorite pheline,
And they both enjoyed the sea-line
    So, they thought, for evermore.

Oh, the days they passed as princes,
Eating chocolate shrimps and quinces,
    Drinking periwinkle wine.
Though he suffered phits and phainted,
Mr. Lear grew well-acquainted
With the landscapes that he painted
    And the cat was doing phine.

But a lady took a notion
To erect between the otion
    And his haven a hotel.
If he could he would have phought her
For the sun and pea-green water,
But he said, "Oh pitter-potter!"
    And he bade a sad pharewell.

The Earl of Derby and

Now out of London town the train
    To Guildford chased the breeze,
Clattering, wheel to windowpane.
    Its passengers were these:

A gentleman, two ladies with
    Two tangled tots in tow,
And last the landscape painter
    You have lately come to know.

Across the aisle, the painter dozed,
    Grinning from ear to ear.
The gent addressed the ladies,
    Tickled silly reading Lear;

"I say, it's good to see," said he,
    "*The Book of Nonsense*. Might
You know who wrote that famous book?"
    Replied the ladies, "Quite!

"Why, Mr. Edward Lear!" they cried.
    "Dear me, a sad mistake,"
The dandy said, sniffing the air,
    "The author is a fake!

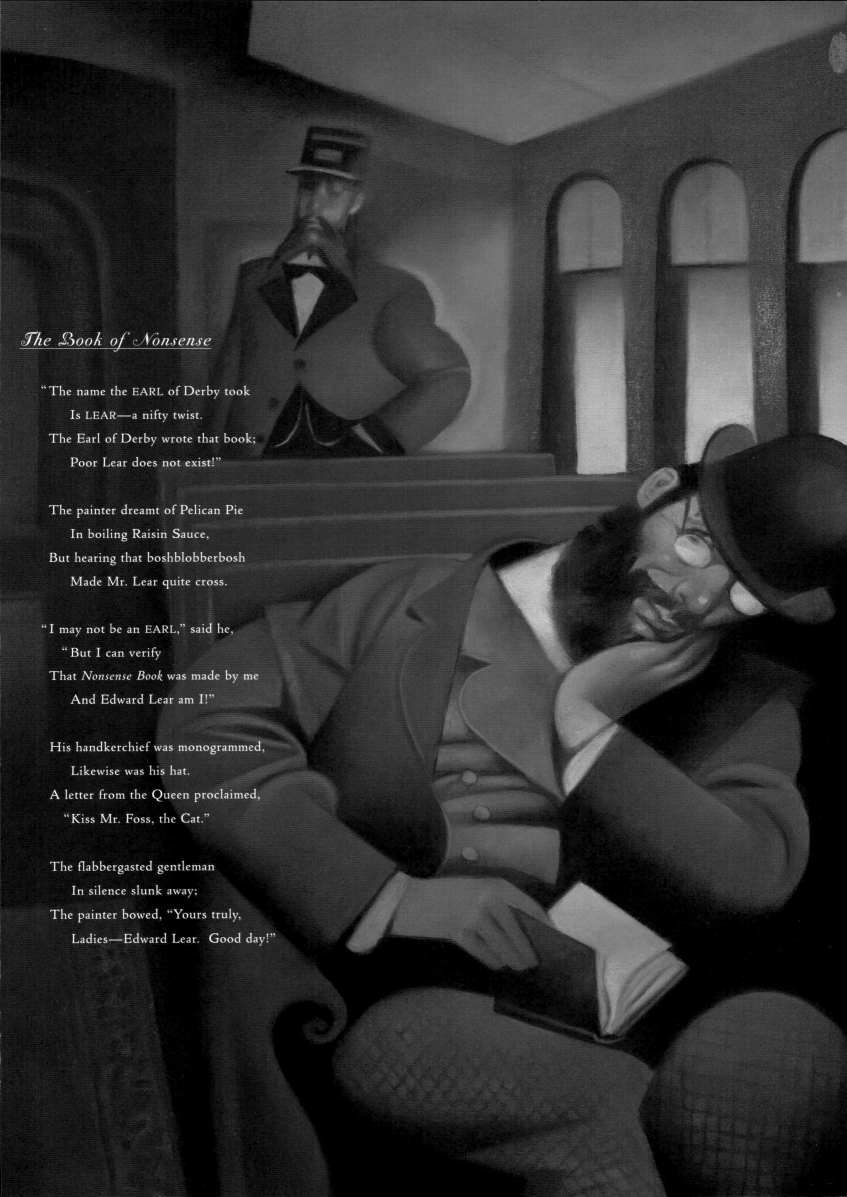

The Book of Nonsense

"The name the EARL of Derby took
    Is LEAR—a nifty twist.
The Earl of Derby wrote that book;
    Poor Lear does not exist!"

The painter dreamt of Pelican Pie
    In boiling Raisin Sauce,
But hearing that boshblobberbosh
    Made Mr. Lear quite cross.

"I may not be an EARL," said he,
    "But I can verify
That *Nonsense Book* was made by me
    And Edward Lear am I!"

His handkerchief was monogrammed,
    Likewise was his hat.
A letter from the Queen proclaimed,
    "Kiss Mr. Foss, the Cat."

The flabbergasted gentleman
    In silence slunk away;
The painter bowed, "Yours truly,
    Ladies—Edward Lear. Good day!"

Old Foss (the Cat) Recalls
His Life with Mr. Lear

You'd say when we ate a late breakfast
    Of jelly or jam in a jar,
"A sliver of ham is upon your pajamas,
    How perfectly messy you are!"

I'd bury my head in your pillow,
    Falling flat in the fold of the fluff.
You'd curse at the blanket and suddenly yank it
    Away, but I knew it was bluff.

And the mice I would catch in the garden—
    Or trap in the trunk of a tree—
I wish had been fatter. "Oh what does it matter?"
    You said, "won't you share them with me?"

Once the postman delivered a letter
    With a ding and a dong on the door.
You replied to that twaddle by vinegar bottle
    And pushed it away from the shore.

After forty-four thousand adventures
    Afoot and afloat and afar,
"One more trip in a tub'll be nothing but trouble,"
    You said. "Let us stay where we are."

And we did. And I say with a sniffle—
    Oh piffle and puffle and posh!—
Although you are minus the title *Your Highness*,
    I bow to the King of High Bosh.

In the Kingdom of Lear

There lived a young man in the Kingdom of Lear
Who laughed at himself as impossibly queer.
He found it amusing to count all his toes;
His arm nearly reached to the end of his nose.
The coat he had fetched from the Tiniskoop Hills
Wore buttons of brass Nicodemus's Pills.
He'd lunch on a bunch of unmunchable crumbs
And dine on rich vittles which punished his gums.
Some thought him as mad as a runcible cat
For living alone in the kingdom like that.
But year after year children came by the score,
When **Nonsense!** he shouted, they shouted for more,

More,

More,

More!

There was nothing so much that they wanted to hear
For they loved that old man in the Kingdom of Lear.

End Notes

Special thanks to my friend and fellow Learicist, Myra Cohn Livingston, for encouraging me to use this title—and for so much more.

Born in a Crowd: Edward Lear, born 1812, was indeed the twentieth of twenty-one children. His father, a London stock-broker, and his weary mother had little time to spend with their ever-growing family. The eldest child, Ann, twenty-two years older than Edward, became her brother's beloved caretaker. When she died in March 1861, Lear wrote to his friend Chichester Fortescue, "I shall be terribly alone." And later he would say, "What I should have been unless [Ann] had been my mother I dare not think." She left what little she had to him: less than 450£, her gold watch, and a brooch which held a lock of her grandmother's hair. Susan Chitty, *That Singular Person Called Lear,* Atheneum, 1989, pp. 188 and 270-71.

The Creatures Wearing Clothes: By the time he was sixteen, Lear had decided to earn his living as a painter. The parrot family was his first specialty. An 1835 painting of the Zoological Gardens at Regent's Park, where he made some of his first sketches, appears in Susan Hyman's *Edward Lear's Birds,* William Morrow & Co., 1980, p. 17.

The Queen Takes Drawing Lessons: In 1846 Lear published his *Illustrated Excursions in Italy.* When Queen Victoria saw the book, she invited him to give her a series of twelve drawing lessons. During one of his visits, the Queen was showing Lear some of the royal treasures. Unable to contain his excitement, he burst out, "I say, where did you get these?" The Queen replied, "I inherited them, Mr. Lear." Vivien Noakes, *Edward Lear: The Life of a Wanderer,* William Collins Sons & Co., Ltd., 1969, p. 55.

Letter By Numbers . . . : Chichester Fortescue—or "My Dear 40scue," as Lear sometimes greeted him in his letters—was one of the poet's lifelong friends. Lear's letters (and journals) are every bit as whimsical as his poems. He took the writing of humorous letters very seriously, inventing all manner of preposterous names for people, places, and things. "What my letters are to you I can't say," he wrote to Fortescue in 1861, "for I never read them over,—but I believe they would be quite as fit to read 100 years hence as any body else's naughty biography, specially when written off hand as mine are." Vivien Noakes, ed., *Edward Lear: Selected Letters,* Oxford University Press, 1990, p. xi.

A Day in the Life . . . A Night in the Life: As Myra Cohn Livingston notes in her *How Pleasant to Know Mr. Lear,* Holiday House, 1982, p. xii: "Lear's search for love is re-echoed in much of his work, but particularly in 'The Courtship of the Yonghy-Bonghy-Bò.' Here is a creature with an absurd name, little in the way of worldly goods, rejected by the Lady Jingly. Initially, ['The Courtship . . .'] may appear to be a funny poem with nonsensical names, but one has only to know some-thing of Lear's life—of how he burst into tears when singing and playing this on the piano—to feel its underlying sadness."

Aboard the SS <u>Coffee-Cup</u>: "The Owl and the Pussy-cat went to sea/In a beautiful pea-green boat," and the Jumblies "went to sea in a Sieve, they did." Though Lear dispatched his imaginary animals over the ocean far and wide and often traveled by steamer himself, he was not enthusiastic about sea voyages. In September 1875, he wrote to Lord Aberdare, "I have hired a pestilential porpuss to cross the Channel as I am too horridly afraid of the sea, & I wont go in the Castalia—as I know it would split & I should fall into the sea between the geminiferous particles." Noakes, ed., *Selected Letters,* p. 249.

In the Middle of Your Face: Lear was forever poking fun at the size of his nose. In a letter to his friend, Evelyn Baring (Lord Cromer), he wrote, "I have sent for 2 large tablecloths to blow my nose on, having already used up all my handkerchiefs." *Edward Lear, The Complete Nonsense Book,* edited by Lady Strachey, Dodd, Mead & Co., 1942, p. 14.

"There once was a man who could cook" : Lear especially enjoyed the "celestially good food" prepared by his life-long servant, Giorgio Cocali, but that did not stop him from concocting his own "Nonsense Cookery," which included his original recipes for Amblongus Pie, Gosky Patties, Crumbobblious Cutlets, and other delicacies.

"There was an Old Man of Dundee" : "Fizzgiggious fish"? What are they? Or "Bong trees" or "calico pies"? Who can say? In poems, letters, and journals, Lear took the greatest delight in inventing new words. For a collection of them, see Myra Cohn Livingston, *A Learical Lexicon,* Margaret K. McElderry Books, 1985.

"That man with the battering ram'll" : In a letter to his sister Ann (January 16, 1849), Lear complained at length about camels. "The sort of horrible way in which they growl & snarl if you only go 6 feet near them—is quite frightful—& if you did not know them—you would suppose they were going to eat you. They do the same to their own masters the Arabs—& appear to have the most unsociable disposition in the world—even among themselves . . . They all seem to say—'Oh! bother you! can't you leave me alone!'" Noakes, ed., *Selected Letters,* p. 99.

"There once was a man who loved vowels" : Lear had a special affection for birds. On June 3, 1848, during one of his many journeys to discover new landscapes for his paintings, he wrote to his sister Ann from Athens: "Owls, the bird of Minerva, are extremely common, & come & sit very near me when I draw." Noakes, ed., *Selected Letters,* p. 77.

Finding Paradise (and Losing It): On October 24, 1878, Lear wrote: "All the trees or nearly all below my ground are cut down—and I heard today that the hotel is to be the largest in San Remo. It is possible that it will hide all my sea-view. But I do not allow myself to think of this ugly affair." In fact, Lear thought endlessly about it. Eventually he moved from his Villa Emily to a new house, Villa Tennyson. Peter Levi, *Edward Lear,* Scribner, 1995, p. 303.

The Earl of Derby and *The Book of Nonsense:* "The temptation was too great to resist," Lear said, "so, flashing all these articles at once . . . I speedily reduced him to silence." His own drawing of this encounter on the train with the doubting gentleman appears in John Lehmann's *Edward Lear and His World,* Charles Scribner's Sons, 1977, p. 47.

Old Foss (the Cat) Recalls His Life with Mr. Lear: Edward Lear died on January 29, 1888. Foss, his closest companion, preceded him in death by three months. Lear had acquired Foss as a kitten in November 1872. On the cat's headstone in Lear's garden, the inscription reads: "Here lies buried my good cat Foss. He was 30 years in my house, and died on 26 November 1887, at the age of 31." Lear was either confused or exaggerating. Foss was sixteen rather than thirty-one when he died. Noakes, ed., *Selected Letters,* p. 313.

In the Kingdom of Lear: The Tiniskoop Hills and Nicodemus's Pills are Mr. Lear's own inventions. Did they actually exist? Of course . . . in the fanciful kingdom of Bosh. A century ago children delighted in reading his nonsense verses. The same is true today. And unless the world a century from now has gone completely to the "mad bad sad," it is a safe bet that "hennyboddy" will be "partickly" enchanted by the nonsense of the once and future King of High Bosh.